The Book of Pithy Sayings
& Quotes of
"Wisdom Pearls "

by LaVerne P. Spruill, Lady L,

Lady Verne

&

The Friends of the Magnet
Exchange Group & Life Changing
Alliances Communities

Preface

Content Contributors

Lady L

Lady Verne

LaVerne Spruill

*Success Beyond Strategz
Enterprise, LLC*

*Craig "Mr. Trillionzzzz' Buchan,
Magnet Exchange Group*

*Kemp, "Mr. Motivator Satchell, Life
Changing Alliances*

*Donald "The Velvet Voice"
Bernardin, Major Alliances*

Content Contributors

William "King William III" Parker,
Haul-Across Perspectives, Inc.

Darlaina Rose,
Healing House of Roses

Bridgette Yelder,
Life Changing Alliances

LaTonja Muhammad,
Magnet Exchange Group

Dr. Deidre Lynn,
Life Changing Alliances

David Terry, King's Court,
Magnet Exchange Group

"BE"

Be Openable   Be Teachable

Be Coachable   Be Flexible

Be Trainable   Be Adaptable

Be Learnable

Lady L

Business Strategz &

Tips with Lady L Show

"Respect Value"

In People

In Resources

In Opportunities

Lady L

There are Dimensions to Purpose

"For every decade of your life, there is another dimension to your purpose. It is YOUR responsibility to discover it, work it, master its skills and give it to the world.

You are a steward of Purpose. God entrusted gifts, talents and calling to you to bless others as well as yourself. Humbly, boldly and with courage, accept the challenge and be about the Father's business."

LadyVerne

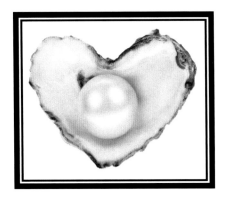

The Power Hidden Within Adversity

"Adversity is a part of the process of growth, to develop strength and wisdom. No resistance, no strength is built. "

LaVerne Spruill

Loyalty

"Be Loyal to YOU First so you can understand Loyalty to someone else."

LaVerne Spruill

Wealth

"Your wealth lies within the fullfilling of your Purpose and Your Passion".

LadyVerne

Solve a Problem

"If YOU can solve a problem,

If YOU can be a solution and

If YOU can be the Answer,

YOU can become

A Millionaire in America."

LaVerne Spruill

Excuses

"Your excuses will keep you in poverty in every area of your life."

Lady L

Change

"Change is good and necessary for growth."

Lady L

MANNERS

"Manners Still Matter"

Lady L

Knowledge

"Knowledge given to me to apply is like......
...a good sauce for my ribs".

Lady L

Kindness

"Kindness is King,

so rule your Kingdom

by

Giving It Away"

Lady L

"Have A:

    Fresh Start Monday

    Tackle It Tuesday

    Work -It -Out Wednesday

    Thankful Thursday

    Finish Strong Friday

    Successful Saturday

    Appreciative, Worshipful Sunday

      Kind of Week"

From the Business Strategz
& Tips With Lady L Show

"To be successful in life you must settle in on this principle:

I am comfortable with being uncomfortable".

Success Beyond Strategz, LLC

Education

"Get Educated, to Stop Being Intimidated"

Lady L

Work

"Work with the Willing"

Success Beyond Strategz, LLC

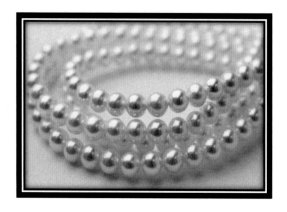

"It's Better to Have it and not Need it, than to Need it and not Have it".

Lady Verne

*"Make Sure You Are
In The Right Boat
With The Right Folk"*

Lady L

"Stop looking back and trippin' over what's behind you."

Stop stressing over what you can't change, fix or un-do.

Stop going forward and trippin' over what is in your past. Let it GO!!"

Mr. Trillionzzz,

Crypto GodFather of the Magnet Exchange Group

"Wealth is a state of mind, FIRST.

It must be seen BEFORE it gets into your bank account."

Mr. Trillionzzz,

Crypto GodFatherz of the Magnet Exchange Group

"If you think the price of winning is too high,

wait until you see the bill you will pay for regret."

Mr. Trillionzzz,

Crypto GodFatherz of the Magnet Exchange Group

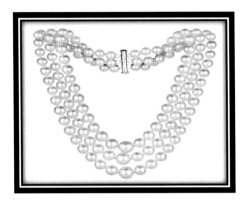

"Take control of YOUR life

Because if you don't,

Someone else will,

And I promise you,

You will not like it."

**Kemp "Mr. Motivator"
Satchell, CEO**

*Life Changing Alliances
(LCA)*

"When facing choices and decisions in your life, especially financial choices and decisions,

Ask yourself these 3 questions:

1. Does it make sense?
2. Does it make sense to me?
3. Do I have the resources and the resolve to finish?

Donald "The Velvet Voice" Bernardin, CEO of Major Alliances, & A CryptoGodFatherz of The Magnet Exchange Group

"Do What You Can, When You Can, While You Can,"

King William III,

CEO of Haul-Across Perspectives, Inc. & a Crypto GodFatherz of The Magnet Exchange Group

Life

"Life is to be Lived NOT Tolerated"

LadyVerne

Wealth

"God put EVERYTHING we will every need in this Earth BEFORE He put man in it.

It's how YOU obtain it for yourself and your families generationally that defines wealth for YOU."

Lady L

Grateful Gratitude

*"You cannot be
GENUINELY thankful
and grateful and be hateful
at the same time."*

Lady L

Poverty

"My War Against Poverty is Real

But I WIN!!!!!!!!"

LaVerne Spruill

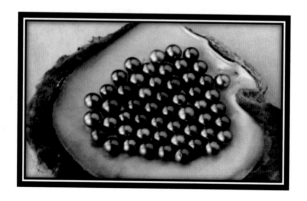

Words

*"Stick and stones can break
your bones and words can
kill your dreams
if you let them."*

Lady L

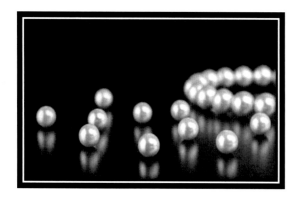

Servant Leadership

"Servants become leaders and leads with Service."

Find a way to SERVE!

Lady L

One of the Queens of the Magnet Exchange Group

Directions

"You can DIRECT" a Horse to the water but you can't make them drink it so stop chasing people with opportunities that will change their lives for the better that they are not open to listen to and to get the information to make a quality, educated decision, especially if it requires effort and some activity on their part."

Lady L via King Donald
"The Velvet Voice" Bernardin,

CEO of Major Alliances, & CryptoGodFatherz of The Magnet Exchange Group

Repetition

"Consistent Repetition of the right thing is the true mother of invention, innovation and creativity."

LadyVerne

*"You are your
Ancestors
wildest dreams"*

Darlaina Rose, *CEO of*

The Healing House of Roses

*"My Mind is a tool and
I Use it, As I wish"*

Darlaina Rose, CEO of

The Healing House of Roses

Learnable

"Don't be a
"Know-it-all" but
Be a "Learn-it-all" and
One who
APPLIES-it-all".

Lady L

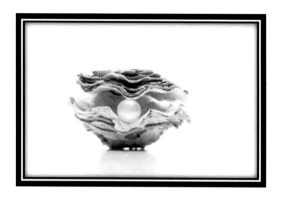

"Start using your mind as a tool instead of it coming against you as a weapon"

Mr. Trillionzzz,

The CryptoGodFather of the Magnet Exchange Group

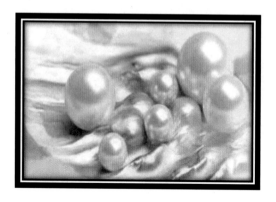

"I'm Grateful to Be Grateful"

Bridgette Yelder

*Member of the
Life Changing Alliances
Group*

(LCA)

"I'm Shifting From Laboring to Creating!"

Bridgette Yelder

Member of the
Life Changing Alliances
Group

(LCA)

"Purpose-filled Practices Produce Profitable Performances."

Lady L

From the Business Strategz & Tips With Lady L" Show

"Don't ever come out of any
trouble and not apply the
wisdom that trouble's
lessons have taught.

You will repeat it, again
until you get it, guaranteed.

Don't do that to yourself! "

Lady L

"*Excuses are tools of incompetence used to build monuments of nothingness.*

Those who specializes in them, seldom specialize in anything else!"

Author Unknown

Brought to the Magnet Exchange Group Community by Member,
LaTonja Muhammad

"*Turn WORRY into WORK*"

Lady L

Success Beyond Strategz Enterprise, LLC

"If you want to change someone's level of passion, help them change their level of knowledge."

Dr. Deidre Lynn, COO
Life Changing Alliances
(LCA)

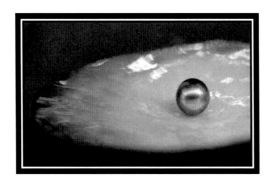

"You've heard the saying, "You can't teach an old dog, new tricks".

The truth is you can't teach a know-it-all new tricks."

LadyVerne

"Be the best that you can be in every situation, every day, in every way.

Strive for personal excellence, Every day"

King William III

CEO of Haul-Across Perspectives, Inc. & CryptoGodFatherz of The Magnet Exchange Group

"Trip going forward because you are one step closer to your goal."

King William III

CEO of Haul-Across Perspectives, Inc. & CryptoGodFatherz of The Magnet Exchange Group

Self-Deception

"The worst deception in the entire world is self-deception; when you allow the enemy of your very own soul to convince you, to lie to yourself and bring destruction to your own human personhood."

Lady L

Favor and Faithfulness

"Favor is for the Faithful"

Lady L via Mr. Trillionzzz,
The CryptoGodFather of
The Magnet Exchange Group

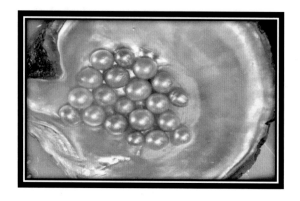

Success

"Success just wants to know,

"How Bad Do You Want It?"

David "The Elder" Terry

King's Court, Magnet Exchange Group

Great Ideas

You've heard the saying, "Great ideas are like catching slippery fish with your hands." Well, if you don't want to lose them, use a net:

"WRITE IT DOWN QUICK"

Lady L

Special Thanks

I give special thanks to every contributor of this book, every quote that I held personally dear to my heart, I was compelled to write and share with the world.

Every quote deserved to be shared.

I hope these "Wisdom Pearls" & Quotes blesse you as much and more than they blessed me and touches your heart with encouragement, courage, clarity, strength, healing and wholeness.

As You read these "Pearls of Wisdom" Calls to Action let them encourage you to quickly apply them to your life so that the difference you seek manifests and add to your life's journey causing you to step out and fulfill your God-given purpose.

The Book of Pithy Sayings & Quotes of "Wisdom Pearls"

by LaVerne P. Spruill, Lady L, Lady Verne

The Friends of the Magnet Exchange Group &

Life Changing Alliances Communities

Made in the USA
Columbia, SC
23 June 2023

18837347R00033